D0012617

THINGS TO DO NOW THAT YOU'RE RETIRED

things to do now

JANE GARTON   Illustrations by Robyn Neild

that you're
retired

spruce

contents

activity rules

Throw away your alarm clock. Get up when you wake up, whatever the time.

Make the effort to get out and about – go to the cinema, that party, the exhibition or the ballet. Get your hair cut, go shopping and mingle with others.

Indulge in little rituals that you enjoy, such as a cappuccino and croissant for breakfast in your local café.

Live for today. No one knows if there'll be a tomorrow, so make the most of every day and enjoy every minute.

Make friends with time. It is your best resource.

You are not past your sell-by date. Think about it ...
you can now fill your life with the things you want to do rather than those you used to have to do.

" *Think left and think right and think low and think high. Oh, the thinks you can think up if only you try.* "
DR SEUSS

Plan your day. Adding some structure to it, with a mixture of chores and relaxation, can make the hours fly by. Planning also helps you focus on the job in hand.

Do different things from day to day. That way, you won't get bored and will always have something new to look forward to.

Keep a diary. Fill it with things to do weeks and even months ahead. Make appointments with yourself and make sure you keep them.

Ring the changes. Altering the way you do things from time to time keeps your brain sharp. Brush your teeth with the hand you don't usually use, take alternate routes to the shops, read a different newspaper.

Make a photo collage of all the important people in your life, past and present, and put it somewhere prominent.

Compile your own cookery book. It's so easy – just write down all of the recipes that you love and they'll be there for posterity to feast on.

Unleash the artist within you. Get out your crayons and sketch away – you don't have to be a budding Damien Hirst.

Buy a painting-by-numbers book and go wild with crazy patterns and shades. It's not just fun for kids.

Is there an unfinished novel lurking in your bottom drawer? Get it out, finish it and send it to publishers and agents. Remember that Mary Wesley had her first novel, *Jumping the Queue*, published shortly after her 70th birthday.

For the ignorant, old age is as winter; for the learned, it is a harvest.
JEWISH PROVERB

Speak the lingo. It's never too late to learn a new language and studies show that the over-50s are just as good at language learning as the young ones. Oui! You can parler français.

Join a national political party and become a campaigner. Or put yourself up for election to your local council.

Think about a refresher driving course to make sure your motor skills are up to scratch.

Make time for the things that make you feel good and you will feel good about the things you do.

Age is a question of mind over matter.
If you don't mind it doesn't matter.
SATCHEL PAIGE

Play games that test your mental recall such as Scrabble, Risk or Trivial Pursuit.

Learn a poem, verse by verse, day by day. Or look at a picture then turn it over and see how many of the objects in it you can remember.

Tease your brain with crosswords, codewords, Sudoku and quizzes, and feel a sense of achievement in completing them.

Avoid CRAFT (can't remember a flipping thing) moments by boosting your mind power with games such as chess and draughts.

Sharpen up your mental powers with a spot of mental arithmetic. Fifteen minutes a day spent solving numerical problems will keep your brain ticking like a Swiss watch, say the experts.

Return to the games of your childhood. Hangman or Battleships always amuse and the grandchildren will love them.

Read or reread all the classics. You may be in for a surprise if it's first time round; you may interpret them differently if it's second time round.

Buy a journal and start a 'Dear Diary'. It will get your creative juices flowing and words on a page can bring back happy memories later on.

Chew gum. Research shows that it can improve both long-term and short-term memory. No one knows exactly why but it's thought that it may improve the delivery of oxygen to the brain.

Become a stargazer. Buy a telescope and tune in to the Milky Way – you may even catch a shooting star.

Spend some time in your local court to see how the judicial system operates.

Start a new garden, planting and harvesting in tune with the lunar cycle. It's called biodynamic gardening.

Want to find out more about nutrition, history of art or gardening? Don't let age stand in your way.

Find out about adult education classes — there are often reduced fees for the over-50s.

Sit on a swing, build a sandcastle, blow bubbles, splash in puddles — anything playful will help to keep you young.

Don't wait for DVDs to come out. You've got time to go to early evening films now. Form a cinema club with family or friends and make it a weekly event. Look out for special cheap film screenings for the over-6os.

'Only connect' as E. M. Forster said. Help yourself to remember by word association. For example, memorize the name of your new friend Patience by visualizing a pack of cards.

Beware of napping, drinking or eating too much, or slumping in front of the TV. If you are guilty of any of the above you could become another couch potato. Change bad habits fast.

Remember your daily schedule no longer needs to run on office time. You can have lunch at three o'clock if you feel like it.

Make sure your home is as comfy as can be. Replace those worn-out sofas and fraying carpets, and if the kitchen dates back more than 15 years maybe it's time to consider a makeover.

Go shopping. Retail therapy is wonderfully effective — as long as you don't spend too much!

Listen to some music if you're feeling down. It's a proven way to lift your spirits and unlike antidepressants has no side effects.

Learn to use a computer, explore the different softwares available. There are plenty of guides for the nervous and technophobic. If you still can't get to grips with technology, enrol in a class for beginners.

Don't become a slave to the TV. Set the video or DVD to record what you want to watch, and enjoy them at a time that suits you.

Work out what you want to do rather than what you have to do. Make time for 'want tos' rather than 'should dos'.

Good at DIY? Why not become a local handyman or handywoman? You'll be the most popular person in the street and it could boost your bank account as well.

If you've always wanted to have your ears pierced or get a tattoo, go ahead! Why not mark a milestone birthday by having it done?

You are own your boss at last. Give yourself orders, but make them achievable.

If your house is too big but you don't want to sell, how about setting up a bed and breakfast or taking in lodgers or students?

Buy a very old car and bring it back to life, then have great fun showing it off to friends.

Invest in a good bird guide and get twitching. Put up a bird table where you can see it and watch your visitors.

Visit all the gardens open to the public in your area. Gen up on plant names before you go so you know what to look out for.

*Knitting is the new yoga –
and it's not just for grannies.
Look out for local purl 'n'
pal or stitch and bitch clubs
and get clicking.*

*Do something for someone else. Search out
volunteering opportunities. You could find yourself
teaching in an orphanage in India, cleaning a
beach in Africa or helping at the 2012 Olympics.*

Avoid situations that make you feel your age. Going clubbing, looking for clothes in the teen section or gatecrashing your grandchildren's parties is guaranteed to make you feel old. Don't go there.

Start scrapbooking. Unearth those boxes of photos and create an album or two! Join a scrapbooking club or enrol in a class to learn more about techniques.

" Give a man a fish and he eats for a day. Teach him how to fish and you get rid of him for the whole weekend. "
ZENNA SCHAFFER

Learn how to tie flies, join your local angling club and catch your first fish.

Move to the beat. Take up the guitar, piano or drums, join a church or community choir and attend local concerts.

Have a siesta. Research shows that your breathing slows down and your blood pressure drops when you nod off, both of which are good for your heart. But keep it short or it could interfere with your night-time sleep.

Become active in your community. Get involved in amateur dramatic productions. Join committees. Launch a church or community newsletter.

" Don't simply retire from something; have something to retire to. "
HARRY EMERSON FOSDICK

" *Retire. Now it is your time to:*
Experience all that life has to offer,
Take time to smell the roses,
Investigate your hobbies,
Revitalize your dreams, and
Embark on a new way of life! "
CATHERINE PULSIFER

Start keeping a folder of special things that cheer you up when you look at them ... important letters, tickets and menus from memorable nights out, newspaper articles that made you laugh, etc.

Get passionate about something that makes you want to do it whenever you can. Then you'll always have something to get out of bed for in the morning.

Find out about ikebana. It's how the Japanese arrange flowers and is based on balance, harmony and form.

Make someone's day sunny by giving them a huge smile.

Be spontaneous and book a tandem for the afternoon. There's a saying that people can be divided into three groups – those who make things happen, those who watch things happen and those who wonder what happened. Doing something different puts you firmly in the first category.

Hold a jumble sale or book a spot at a car-boot sale and get rid of all your junk.

Step out with a pedometer. Some local councils dispense them for free now. Aim for 10,000 steps a day eventually.

Find out what was happening on the day you were born. The Internet would be a good place to start. Alternatively, leaf through old magazines in libraries and remember what life was like in your teens.

Always hankered after the big screen? Register with an agency that provides extras for films and TV – people of all ages, shapes and sizes are needed. You never know – you could end up in a blockbuster!

Make a list of all the things you've never done in your life, then do them just because you've never done them!

Don't put yourself under pressure. You really don't have to finish those letters now or mow the lawn today. You have all the time in the world, so take advantage of it.

" I have no patience with people who grow old at 60 just because they are entitled to a bus pass. It should be the time to start something new, not put your feet up. "
MARY WESLEY, NOVELIST

recharge
yourself

Walk tall. Imagine you're being pulled up like a puppet by a piece of string from the middle of your head. Good posture helps you feel young and protects against aches and pains.

Get on your bike – a 20-minute ride boosts metabolism by 29 per cent for up to an hour. It also gets you out in the fresh air.

Strengthen your core muscles with Egyptian bellydancing (or, to give it its proper name, Raqs Sharqi). It strengthens and stretches the muscles in your stomach, back, thighs and pelvic floor, helping you to look longer and leaner.

Look on the bright side and think colorful – in your clothes, flowers or home. Here are some of the best for vitality.
- *Yellow stimulates mental activity.*
- *Orange boosts energy and appetite.*
- *Reds and bright pinks promote physical activity.*

Stretch away tiredness by reaching up above your head with your fingertips. Shrug your shoulders up and down, then clasp your hands behind your back to release shoulderblade tension and have a good yawn.

Try power walking. You can do it anytime, anywhere and it really gets your heart beating.

Take a look at your forehead. Too many wrinkles for your liking? Your digestive system could be sluggish. Drink more water to improve your circulation.

269 calories – that's the number you could burn by massaging your partner before bed.

Make a list of all the things you need to do and seize the moment. Choose one thing and do it.

Commune with nature. Being outdoors has an automatic grounding effect. It will help you slow down, reconnect with the earth and get things in perspective.

Keep a vase of flowers where you can see them. They'll give you and the atmosphere an instant lift.

Try working out on a Swiss ball. The first time you sit on one you'll wobble like a jelly, but they are fantastic for building core stability the gentle way. Most come with exercise guides or you could ask a personal trainer to devise a routine for you.

Feeling sluggish? Close your eyes and take five deep breaths wherever you are. It will get more oxygen flowing to the brain and fill you with energy.

Keep moving, but ease into exercise slowly and be kind to your body. Don't kick off your regime with a 30-minute run. Instead, start with five minutes' walking. Then add one minute per day until you reach your 30-minute-a-day goal.

Choose a gym that's not far from home. You need to conserve your energy for the activity, not the getting there – research shows that if a gym is more than 10 minutes away you won't use it as much as you should.

Try small exercises while doing other things. Do a couple of knee bends while you're on the phone or try pulling in your tummy muscles while driving or standing in a supermarket queue.

Exercise with others – the social side will help keep you motivated.

Get out in the sunshine – it's good for you. It will boost your spirits and help build up stores of vitamin D, needed for strong bones and teeth. But don't forget to use sunscreen, with an SPF of at least 15.

Of course you can run a marathon or do a bungee jump, but gently does it. If you haven't exercised for a while, build up to it gradually. Yoga or aqua fitness classes are a good way to start.

Be an a.m. exerciser. Go jogging at dawn or have an early morning dip in the sea. See if they do tai chi in your local park.

Try tai chi. Its controlled, gentle moves are ideal if your joints are starting to play up, as it puts no pressure on your body. It can have an incredibly calming effect on mind and body.

Why do people love Pilates? To give you a hint, its low-impact moves focus on strengthening the core muscles that support your spine and pelvis.

Put on your swimming costume and do some aquarobics. In studies, women who exercised in water were found to have reduced heart rate and blood pressure compared with those who worked out on land.

Dance the night away. Play something with a strong rhythm and let your body leap, bend, twist and spin to the beat. Do whatever comes naturally. When you're worn out, lie on the floor to cool down and enjoy the wonderful feeling of contentment.

Put on your most-loved tune at home or in the car and exercise those vocal cords. Singing boosts happiness because it makes you breathe more deeply, which means more oxygen reaches your muscles and you start to relax and wind down.

Kites aren't just for kids. Buy one or make your own and head to the hills. It's a great way to burn energy in the big outdoors.

Burn an extra 100 calories a day:
- *Play footie for 15 minutes.*
- *Walk briskly for 16 minutes.*
- *Vacuum the house for 20 minutes.*
- *Walk up and down stairs for 10 minutes.*
- *Wash and polish the car for 20 minutes.*

You've worked hard for years.
Now it's time to play hard.

Re-educate yourself in the
art of standing, sitting and
moving with the Alexander
Technique. Be prepared to
exercise lying down with a pile
of books under your head.

Play ping-pong. You need to play it fast and concentrate, which is great for improving coordination and reaction time.

Get yourself a mini-trampoline and bounce away to your heart's content. It will help strengthen your bones without straining your joints.

Put on your wellies and get gardening. Wielding the hoe and strimming the edge of the lawn are great alternatives to a sweaty tone-up class in the gym.

Save your energy.
Put down heavy bags
whenever you can and
park as close as possible
to your destination even
if it means paying for a
parking space.

*Keep trying new sports. You're
never too old and the wider the
range of challenges and activities
you engage in, the more people you
will meet and the more skills you
will learn. How about windsurfing,
running or archery for starters?*

Climb to the top of a mountain. One fifth of the world's surface is covered in mountains, so you shouldn't have too much trouble finding one.

Plant a tree. You'll be helping the environment and creating a living memorial to yourself. Your family might enjoy it in years to come.

Learn to skim stones (some people call it 'playing ducks and drakes'). It's free and all you need is a flat stone and lots of water. Once you get the knack, it can be hard to stop.

Give up technology for a week and recharge YOUR batteries. Go without e-mails and texts and talk to people face to face for a change.

Bungee-jump! No, you're never too old. Head off to the bridge over the Bloukrans River in South Africa for the ultimate energizing experience.

Energy is the power that drives every human being. It is not lost by exertion but maintained by it.
GERMAINE GREER

Feel the force of magnet therapy. Magnets work on the cells deep within your body, clearing out waste products and helping boost immunity. Invest in a magnet mattress pad, wear a bracelet, or try some patches.

Get your circulation going with some home hydrotherapy. First take a hot shower (as hot as you can bear without scalding) for three minutes, then turn the shower to cold for four minutes. Alternate three to four times.

Don't bottle up stress – laugh, scream, shout, swear; do anything that helps you let it all out.

Get the needle. Release your energy reserves with acupuncture. A short course helps stimulate the body's natural healing response, as well as removing any blockages in your energy pathways.

Clear your desk of clutter, then add the following plants to clear pollution from the air: peace lilies, spider plants, philodendrons or sansevieria.

Burn some oils. Basil stimulates a tired brain, rosemary aids concentration, while lemon and bergamot help efficiency.

"It is not wise to rush about ... if too much energy is used, exhaustion will follow."
LAO TZU

Pull on those trainers and get walking. According to research, you can add an hour on to your life for every hour you walk.

Make every day an adventure. When you stop stepping out you are in danger of drying out like an old potato.

out and about

Visit your local airfield and book a flight in a glider to get an aerial view of life.

Learn the flags of different countries.

Keep a travel diary. Buy one or make your own. Fill it with postcards, menus, drink mats, rail tickets … any memento that reminds you of where you have been. It could bring you hours of pleasure later on.

Choose a country that you love and plan a tour of the churches and cathedrals in as many of the major cities as you can visit.

Go to the beautiful Omar Ali Saifuddien Mosque in Brunei, built by the present sultan in memory of his father.

Forget Goa — been there; done that. Spend New Year's Eve camel-watching in the Thar Desert on the India-Pakistan border.

Experience the last days of the Raj – and we don't mean the Indian restaurant. Plan a trip to India incorporating as many sites from the days of English rule as possible. Read the *Raj Quartet* by Paul Scott to inspire you.

Lose yourself in contemplation in front of the Taj Mahal, one of the most romantic monuments in the world.

Take a steamer up Lake Garda, throw pennies in the Trevi fountain in Rome and live la dolce vita.

Hear what the Pope has to say in St Peter's Square, Rome. He holds an open audience on Wednesdays.

Put on your walking boots and go up Table Mountain in Cape Town, South Africa, or Sugarloaf Mountain in Brazil.

Hire a bike and cycle round the war cemeteries in Normandy, France.

Read Captain Corelli's Mandolin *by Louis de Bernières on the beach in Kefalonia, Greece, where it is set.*

Jump on a dawn boat from Athens and ferry-hop around the Cyclades. Don't forget your pan pipes.

See where Barbara Hepworth laid her head, then let her sculptures tower above you in her gardens in St Ives, Cornwall.

Discover why a pinetum is different from an arboretum at the beautiful Nymans Garden in West Sussex.

Reconnect with the environment at the Eden Project in Cornwall … but leave your pooch behind. Dogs are not allowed on the main site.

Want to find out more about climate change, pollution and the state of the planet's resources? Go on-line and explore the sites of Friends of the Earth and Greenpeace.

Put on your dancing shoes – try salsa in Cuba, flamenco in Spain, tango in Buenos Aires and samba in Rio.

Test your fitness levels and sign up for the Steyning Stinger in West Sussex, one of Britain's toughest half-marathons (the less than fit can walk it).

Go to London and pay homage at Samuel Taylor Coleridge's house in Highgate, then follow the masses to Karl Marx's grave in Highgate Cemetery.

Do a spot of grave-gazing at the Père Lachaise cemetery in Paris. There you'll find the headstones of Jim Morrison, Edith Piaf, Oscar Wilde, Max Ernst and Honoré de Balzac, among many other notables.

Hunt for out-of-print books at the Shakespeare and Company secondhand bookshop in Paris. That's where James Joyce used to browse.

Eat a pig's head in Ernest Hemingway's most-loved restaurant Sobrino de Botín, a stone's throw from the Playa Mayor in Madrid.

Find out why Guinness is good for you in its traditional Irish home in Dublin. When you've had your fill, move on to Trinity College Dublin and be illuminated by the Book of Kells.

Head to upstate New York and relive the summer of love at Woodstock, then complete your journey with a few flowers in your hair in San Francisco.

Play 'The Ballad of Lucy Jordan' by Marianne Faithfull as loud as you can 'as you drive through Paris in a sports car with the warm wind in your hair'.

Seek out the specialities of the region you're visiting. Go for 'pasteis de nata' in Lisbon, oysters in Boulogne, pizza in Naples, snails in Paris, and bouillabaisse in Marseilles.

Get a Brazilian in Rio, a bindi in Bangalore and your hair braided in Barbados.

Stock up on saffron in Marrakech, turmeric in India and cinnamon in Sri Lanka.

Be a Shirley Valentine and watch the sun set at Agios Ioannis on the Greek island of Mykonos.

Go camel racing in Dubai or motor racing in Le Mans, chase the bulls in Pamplona and join in the goat dance in Skyros.

Spend Christmas in another country. Escape the city blues for the snowscapes of Switzerland, Austria or Canada. Alternatively, go in search of the sun in the Caribbean.

Learn how to say useful phrases in other languages. There are around 6,700 languages in the world, so that should keep you busy.

Take photos of as many animals in the wild as you can.

Stand on the Equator and experience what it feels like to have one foot on either side of the world.

Go on a shell-finding outing to Scourie beach in Sutherland, Scotland. See how many cowrie shells you can collect.

See the Northern Lights (aurora borealis). The best countries to view from include Canada, Alaska, Greenland, Iceland, Russia and Sweden.

Blindfold your eyes, stick a pin into a map and travel to where it lands. No peeping now!

> Staying young is an attitude. It has nothing to do with how old we are.
> LYNDA FIELD

Get a taste for the high life atop the world's tallest buildings. Try the Canadian National Tower in Toronto, the Oriental Pearl Tower in Shanghai, Sears Tower in Chicago, Taipei 101 in Taipei or the Petronas Towers in Kuala Lumpur.

Go on a pilgrimage to:
- Fatima in Portugal
- Santiago de Compostela in Spain
- Knock in County Mayo, Ireland
- Tinos in Greece.

See how many hot springs you can visit in a year but mind you don't stumble on a hot geyser. The Old Faithful Geyser in Yellowstone National Park, Wyoming, is a must, followed closely by the famous Blue Lagoon in Iceland.

Be a tourist in your home town. Explore the sights on foot and visit all the local galleries and museums.

Skydiving may not be for you but you can still go up, up and away on a balloon safari in East Africa's Masai Mara.

THINGS TO DO NOW THAT YOU'RE RETIRED

The White Towns in Andalusia, Spain, are not called 'white' for nothing. Go and see for yourself. Mind how you walk – the roads are steep and narrow.

Get lost in the maze in Hampton Court Palace, Surrey, then see how many more mazes you can negotiate in a year. We recommend the mazes at:

- Longleat House and Safari Park in Wiltshire.
- Blenheim Palace in Oxfordshire.
- Hever Castle in Kent.
- Vandusen Gardens in Vancouver.
- The Gardens of the Marquis of Alfarras in Barcelona.
- The Pineapple Garden Maze, Dole Plantation in Wahiawa.

Ever wondered what they mean by a boutique hotel? Book yourself in for a no-expenses-spared weekend and see why the rich are different. Indulge at:

- Driftwood, Portscatho, Cornwall.
- Miller's Residence, Notting Hill Gate, London.
- J. K. Place, Florence.
- Casa No. 7, Seville.
- Pavillon de la Reine, Place des Vosges, Paris.

Did you know that you can cycle along Hadrian's Wall? The recently opened track follows the path from the Cumbrian coast to the North Sea. Don't forget to check the flood levels at Solway marshes before you set out.

Admire the ancient cliff faces along the Jurassic coast in Dorset, then focus on fossils at one of the local museums.

Pump adrenaline in Zambia, home of the Victoria Falls. If you're really brave, try tandem skydiving and microlighting for thrills in the air, or white-water rafting and body-boarding in the Zambezi.

Unwind and chill out listening to the soft sounds of reggae music in Ocho Rios, Jamaica. Other star attractions are humming birds, a trip on a bamboo boat, or the chance to explore coffee and tea plantations.

Fancy going somewhere where the sun shines 24/7? Try Reykjavik, the capital of Iceland. You can watch the Northern Lights set the winter skies alight, or go skinny-dipping in a natural geothermically heated pool.

Turtles, stingrays, moray eels, squid and small reef sharks are all on the scuba-diving schedule around the beautiful Caribbean island of Grenada. If you prefer to keep your feet on dry land, there's beach volleyball and archery, plus lively street markets just waiting to be enjoyed.

Pretend to be a cowboy and saddle up for a horseback safari at a South African ranch. If you're lucky you'll see hippos, wildebeeste, wild pigs, zebras, warthogs and rhinos as you ride out.

Pack an easel and paintbrush and go on a passage to India, capturing your holiday on canvas. Play with the shades and tones in Rajasthan – and don't forget to visit the 'blue city' of Jodhpur with its formidable majestic fort.

Discover what inspired Charles Darwin to develop his famous theory of evolution in the Galapagos Islands of Ecuador. The range of flora and fauna will bowl you over.

Head to Vanuatu, an archipelago of 83 islands in the Pacific. According to one study, the people who live there are the happiest on earth, ranking first in the 'Happy Planet Index'. Perhaps if you smile they will share their secret.

Step out of your comfort zone and sleep under canvas for a week. These days, camping can be as basic or as sophisticated as you choose. Just don't forget the foam mattress – your discomfort threshold may not be quite what it used to be.

Mark the start of spring at Varanasi on the banks of the River Ganges. Each year, the festival of Diwali (the festival of light) celebrates the changing seasons with bonfires, dancing and a lot of noise.

Search out animals in their natural habitat – snorkel or dive to see fish, visit a nature reserve, or go on a safari. Swim with dolphins.

Was King Arthur really buried in the abbey grounds? Is the Holy Grail hidden in Chalice Well? There is much more to Glastonbury than the mud-ridden music festival.

Go on a historical tour of the cathedrals dedicated to the Virgin Mary after the Knights Templar returned to France from the Holy Land in the twelfth century. They include Chartres, Rouen, Amiens, Reims, Bayeux, Evreux and Loan.

Book a special access tour to Stonehenge and stand between the giant megaliths – and pretend you are a druid for an afternoon.

Get a bird's-eye view of London on the London Eye ferris wheel. Don't worry – it moves so slowly that you won't feel sick or dizzy.

You only live once …
so visit Golden Eye in
Jamaica, the home of Ian
Fleming. Here you can
see the desk where he
penned many of the James
Bond thrillers.

It can only be reached on horseback
or on foot, but your first glimpse of
Jordan's Petra, the City of the Tombs,
will be enough to reassure you that it
was worth the effort.

Match me a marvel save in Eastern clime,
A rose-red city half as old as time.
JOHN BURGON,
VICTORIAN SCHOLAR, FROM HIS POEM 'PETRA'

Descend in a submersible to see some of the world's famous shipwrecks – the Bismark, the Titanic and even HMS Breadalbane under the Arctic.

Calling all Elvis fans ... go to Memphis and book yourself on a tour of Graceland, the palace of the King of Rock and Roll.

Zoom to Russia on a space tour. Make sure it includes a visit to the Star City Training Centrum, where Russian cosmonauts are trained.

The turquoise coast of Turkey is a must. Visit the famous sunken city of Kekova by sea-kayak, the remains of the Lycian city of Arycanda, and the ruins near Kas.

Set out on a spiritual journey to some of the most sacred energy sites in the world. Meditate on Holy Mount Kailash in Tibet, in the ashrams found all over India, or at Machu Picchu in Peru.

Fancy a flutter? Take a punt on an overseas horse-racing holiday and choose from great events such as the Dubai World Cup, the Melbourne Cup or the Breeder's Cup in the USA.

Feel the thrill and excitement of skydiving on terra firma. 'Bodyflying' takes place in a specially designed wind tunnel. Age is no barrier: you just have to be fit, agile and healthy. Visit www.bodyflight.co.uk for details.

Introduce your grandchildren to the delights of crabbing in the rock pools at Kimmeridge on the Dorset coast. It will keep them quiet for an afternoon and you might come home with crabs for tea!

Travel on the Trans-Siberian Express from Moscow to Beijing. When you come home, you can say you have been on the longest train journey in the world.

Combine holiday and study on a language course in the Pyrenees. You'll return speaking Spanish and looking healthy and fit from all the mountain air.

Swap your French phrase book for a German one and seek the Alpine Riviera in the southern province of Carinthia, Austria. The lakes boast temperatures of up to 27°C (80°F) and there's lots of alfresco dining.

If you're in Mexico, do as the Mexicans do – pop down to the playa. A day out at this beach is more about tacos, Latina pop music and skyscraper views than a lazy few hours in the sun, but it's still worth a visit.

Head for Papafragas Beach on the island of Milos, Greece. The beach is part cave, part natural swimming pool with crystal-clear waters that change color throughout the day. And that's not all – legend says that the area was once a pirate's lair.

Only in Japan: if you can't get to the beach, the beach comes to you. At Miyazaki City in Kyushu, you can take the plunge at the world's largest indoor water park.

Go on a cruise. It's a wonderful way to see the world without having to organize the whys and wherefores. And it's a good meeting opportunity for solo adventurers.

Most travel for seniors is heavily discounted, so find out what's available and make the most of it.

Combine a cookery course with a holiday in destinations ranging from India to Indonesia, Morocco to Mexico or Sydney to Seville. Visit www.holidayonthemenu.com for details.

Take tea at London's Ritz Hotel in Mayfair at least once. And yes, cucumber sandwiches are on the menu plus every type of tea you can think of. Just remember the dress code – jeans and trainers are not allowed.

Make a feathered friend – meet a bird of prey on a falconry course. You'll get to hold a bird and may even do some 'flying'. Visit www.hawkexperience.co.uk for details.

Learn about fine wines and take in some breathtaking scenery on a tour round one of the classic wine regions. Sip on a trip through Burgundy in France, Portugal's Douro Valley and the Rioja area in Spain.

Look out for city-break deals in newspapers. They're good value at off-peak times. Remember to check what is and is not included. If you don't, you could end up with a very big bill.

Celebrate an anniversary or birthday by hiring a stretch limo for the night. Some even have mood lighting and stargazer ceilings. What more could you want?

How about going on a gap year for grown-ups? Fancy trekking through mountains, visiting far-flung places, exploring tropical jungles or working with endangered species? You name it, you can do it. For details, visit www.gapyearforgrownups.co.uk.

Carnival your way across the globe. There's the Rio carnival in Brazil, the Venice Carnivale or the winter carnival in Quebec — and that's just for starters.

Leave your cares behind and hit the open road in a camper van — you never know where it might lead you.

You've seen it in the movies and now you've got the time to do it yourself. We're talking about a coast-to-coast road trip across the USA. Come on, what's 3,000 miles when you've proved you can go the distance?

Show a tourist, around your city and you'll appreciate what's on your own doorstep even more.

And I'd like to roll to Rio some day before I'm old.
RUDYARD KIPLING

" The policy of being too cautious is the greatest risk of all. "
JAWAHARLAL NEHRU

Make getting in touch with the natural world a priority. After all, it's the real thing.

Think about investing in a time-share. Choose the option that gives you access to holiday venues all over the world.

THINGS TO DO NOW THAT YOU'RE RETIRED

Take a course and then do the holiday — study art history and go to Florence; scuba-dive and go to the Great Barrier Reef; take up riding and go to Argentina.

Visit the new Seven Wonders of the World:
- India's Taj Mahal.
- The Great Wall of China.
- Jordan's Petra.
- Brazil's statue of Christ the Redeemer.
- Peru's Machu Picchu.
- Mexico's Chichén Itzá Pyramid.
- Rome's Colosseum.

'Travel back in time to a more gracious era' on the Orient Express. And the good news is you don't have to travel to Venice to enjoy the experience. Day trips will take you from London's Victoria station at a slow pace through the English countryside while you tuck into a five-course lunch with champagne and liqueurs. Visit www.orient-express.com.

Safety on the move. Beware of pickpockets and purse-snatchers. Wear a waist purse. Carrying a whistle can also be a good self-protective move.

See your doctor before you travel. Make sure any prescription medicines you may be taking are legal in the countries you're planning to visit.

Get the biggest suitcase on wheels that you can. Invest in a shooting stick and use it to sit on if the going gets tough.

If you don't have a cell phone, get one now but don't leave it on the kitchen table. Take it with you wherever you go – it will make you feel much safer.

flatter
yourself

You can't stop looking older but you can make the most of what you've got.

Take out a subscription to a health and beauty magazine to inspire you to keep up to date with the latest trends.

There's no getting away from it. Looking good in retirement requires time and money. Decide how much you have of either and how much you want to spend on both, then go for it.

Celebrate your birthdays. Have the 50th birthday party you never had. Remember: 60 is the new 50.

Revamp your image. For ideas, enlist the help of a personal stylist. If your budget won't stretch to that, most department stores now run a free personal shopping service.

Brighten up. Apply pure lemon juice after your moisturizer. It will make your skin look tighter and brighter.

Treat yourself. There's nothing like a facial, a trip to the hairdresser or a day at a health spa to make you feel on top of the world.

Embrace the chocolate counter. A little of what you fancy does you good once in a while. And if you can't enjoy those truffles now, when can you?

Aim to look fabulous and feel fabulous rather than to look 20 again.

Good grooming goes a long way to covering up those wrinkles, sagging or extra pounds.

Grow old gracefully. There's nothing worse than mutton dressed as lamb and nothing better than smart, sophisticated 60-somethings.

Hands are a dead giveaway of age. Make sure yours don't let you down. Wear rubber gloves for washing up and moisturize after every session.

Make a statement. Look out for eye-catching beads and bracelets and bring on the bling!

Prevent bags under your eyes with this instant eye-brightener. Place warm camomile teabags over your eyes for three minutes, then swap them for cool slices of cucumber. Switch between the two to help increase blood flow to the area.

Feed your skin from the inside out with foods rich in vitamin E such as wheatgerm, avocado and eggs.

A facial massage stimulates nerve endings, increases blood flow and helps relieve that age-old cause of wrinkles – tension.

Don't go out without your 'slap'. A little lippy goes a long way.

Recharge your batteries from time to time by booking into a hotel with a spa for a weekend break. Relax, have a massage and just enjoy being pampered.

Get a pet. Stroking cats and dogs is calming, they love you unconditionally, and best of all they don't answer back.

Treat your skin with oils such as frankincense and ylang-ylang to replenish your natural oils. Mix four to eight drops in 50ml (1½ fl oz) of a base oil such as almond.

Slip, slap, slop. Be generous with sunscreen whatever the weather. You need at least 100ml/3fl oz (or ⅓ of a small bottle) to cover the whole body. Don't rub it in too hard or you risk losing some of the protective factor.

To help transport you to the Land of Nod, add lavender oil to a soothing warm bath or put a few drops on your pillow.

Brush up. A spot of skin brushing before your daily shower will strengthen immunity, boost circulation, reduce cellulite and help rid the body of toxins. Use a natural skin brush on dry skin and brush firmly and smoothly, always towards the heart.

Take years off your face in an instant. We're not talking cosmetic surgery, just brow shaping. Tweezing is the easiest way, or you may prefer a professional wax, threading or sugaring.

Get a glowing complexion with selenium or co-enzyme Q10 supplements – both act as powerful antioxidants, protecting and rejuvenating skin.

Wake yourself up with essential oils. Fresh citrus oils such as bergamot and lemon are well known for their mood-lifting effects, especially first thing in the morning. Just put a couple of drops on your hanky and inhale.

Stave off lethargy with the following quick fix. Hold the middle joint of your left middle finger lightly between your right thumb and fingers. Hold for a few moments. Repeat on the other hand and feel an instant energy boost.

Buy shoes at the end of the day, when your feet are slightly larger, to avoid choosing a style that could turn out to be too tight.

To lighten age spots, try this natural remedy: mix together the juice of a lemon, two tablespoons of honey and 60ml (2fl oz) of plain yogurt, and gently massage into skin once a week.

Bring back a youthful glow with an illuminating moisturizer. Look out for one with special light-reflecting pigments, then apply a sheer foundation on top.

How about some hairobics? An Indian head massage will boost blood and lymph circulation, making sure hair follicles are supplied with lots of nutrients and fresh oxygen.

If you have lower back pain, don't lift heavy loads. Ask other people to do it; even get help with the shopping.

Do a one-day detox once a month. Drink a large glass of fruit juice every two hours and as much water as you like throughout the day. It has a cleansing effect and will leave you bubbling with energy.

Give your feet a breather and go barefoot whenever you can. Walking barefoot can also stimulate reflex points on the feet, with beneficial effects throughout the body.

See if you can lift your big toe up and down while holding down your other toes with your hand. It's great for flexibility.

Feeling stressed? Place a moist lavender bag over your eyes and feel the tension ebb away.

Do a Jackie O and slip on some big sunglasses. They add a touch of mystery as well as protecting the eyes from the sun's damaging rays. Make sure they have good UV protection.

Don't wait for a special occasion to smarten up. Dress up whenever you choose and notice how much better you feel.

Stop the clock for at least five minutes once a day. Do absolutely nothing. Just sit and be.

Laugh as much as you can. Three minutes of cheery chortling has as many health benefits as 10 minutes of aerobic exercise, say the experts. It deepens your breathing, triggers the release of endorphins, the body's own happy hormones, and helps keep you positive.

Stay clear of sunbeds. They give off high levels of UV light, which can damage skin and increase your risk of cancer. The only safe tan is the one that comes in a bottle.

Did you know that while you sleep your body goes about its essential work of cell repair and rejuvenation? Make sure you get at least seven or eight hours sleep a night.

Avoid flat shoe syndrome. Wear high heels for special occasions. They can make you look taller and slimmer and are just the thing for showing off good legs. Don't overdo it though – even a small kitten heel is high enough.

Give your nails a weekly manicure. Long talons don't flatter old hands. Shorter nails look better and are less likely to break.

Drink cranberry juice. It's thought to contain chemicals that may help prevent bacteria sticking to your teeth, which can cause cavities. Search for low-sugar varieties.

Focus on warm tones for your make-up, blusher, lip gloss and mascara. It will take years off your look.

To help you get to sleep at night, massage your feet with warmed sesame oil after your bedtime bath.

Feel like everything is going south? A well-fitting bra can help solve the problem. Get measured by professionals.

Buy a rubber ball from your local toyshop and keep it somewhere handy. Squeeze it every time you see it, for at least a minute, to keep your hands strong.

Good posture can make you look slimmer so stand up straight and keep those shoulders back.

> " A face that's not overly
> made up looks younger.
> CATHERINE DENEUVE "

Use tinted moisturizer for daytime cover. It's kinder on lines and wrinkles than foundation and easier to apply.

If your sight is not quite what it used to be, invest in a good magnifying mirror. That way, you'll never miss a blemish.

Reduce fading hair color with a trip to the hairdresser

Give your eyes a morning workout. Tap the undereye area lightly and swiftly with your fingertips, moving from the inner to the outer corner of your eye and back.

Scrape your tongue. A special tongue cleaner can help keep breath sweet and fresh. Alternatively, run an upside-down spoon back and forth across your tongue at the back of your mouth.

Visit the New Age section in your local music shop. Listening to calming music can help you to unwind and relax. If you like plainsong, it does the job just as well.

> "When it comes to make-up, minimalism and subtlety are watchwords."
>
> VICCI BENTLEY,
> BEAUTY WRITER

Keep to your ideal weight. A plump face may make you look younger, but extra pounds increase your risk of heart disease.

Give up smoking. It robs your skin of oxygen and encourages lines and wrinkles. Worse still it increases the risk of breast, cervical and lung cancer.

Make color your ally when it comes to hair. Rich vegetable rinses are gorgeously glossy and conceal the first signs of gray. Highlights near the face lift and flatter skin tone.

Edit your make-up. Sticking to the look you had in your 30s is a common ageing pitfall. Get up to date. Ease up on eye make-up and concentrate instead on warm lip and cheek tones that bring vitality to your face.

Baggy clothes may seem tempting, but slightly fitted designs give your figure structure and help conceal rogue lumps and bumps.

Rethink your hairstyle. Shorter hair lifts features and can be just as effective as a face-lift! On the other hand, if your hair is your crowning glory, who says you can't keep it long – just make sure you get a good cut.

Tired of being told to cheer up? Research facial exercises on the Internet – they can help you reinvent your expression without moving a muscle.

Now you don't have to rush off to work, have sex in the morning. Make-up artists say the energy surge that follows plumps up skin, giving it the freshest kind of afterglow.

Alternate your shoes from day to day. It helps relieve pressure spots as well as keeping muscles and tendons flexible.

Cry out loud. Experts now think that tears may contain stress chemicals — proving that you really can and should sob stress out of your system.

Put your best foot forward with a podiatrist. Bunions, calluses and corns can make life hell, so why put up with them?

Always wear black? Think pink instead and life will be even rosier.

Cut the caffeine. Go on –
just try it for a month. See
how your skin tone changes,
your sleep gets deeper and
you feel more relaxed.

Detox your wardrobe. Give old clothes to charity and sell those you've hardly worn on eBay. It's fun and will help fund the next shopping spree.

Different activities create different moods. Play music loudly, jump up and down, smell essential oils, have a bath, go for a swim. Do what works for you.

Swap the side of the bed you get out of. It could put a whole new perspective on the way you start the day.

Sweat it out in a sauna or steam room. It gets rid of toxins and can help soothe daily aches and pains.

Change your look with a new pair of specs. If you can't make up your mind which frames to go for, take a friend for a second opinion, or ask the optician to help you.

Tap your face in the shower. The rush of blood to your cheeks helps firm your face and leaves you looking fresh and flushed.

Blast areas of orange-peel skin (the dreaded cellulite) with a power shower, using circular movements.

Wear a hat in the sun if you value your face. Those UV rays dry out skin and trigger wrinkles.

stay
well

A little of what you fancy does you good – a couple of glasses of red wine a night can help protect your heart. But no more, or it could have the opposite effect.

Dream on – this is your mind's way of processing the events of the day.

Make a fruit and veg rainbow and eat at least five portions every day - mixing green, yellow, orange, red, purple and white. Each has different vitamins and minerals that your body needs to keep healthy.

To strengthen bones think vitamin D. Sometimes known as the sunshine vitamin, vitamin D is made naturally by your body on exposure to the sun. Expose some area of your skin, such as your face and hands, to daylight at least twice a day for 10 minutes. Good food sources include oily fish such as salmon and mackerel, eggs and margarine.

To get rid of tension in your neck and shoulders, try this. Sitting upright in a comfortable chair, lower your head until your chin rests on your chest, then slowly raise it again. Repeat a few times, making sure you breathe slowly and evenly throughout.

Risk bad breath and include garlic in your diet as much as you can. It contains antioxidants that can help boost your immune system. It may also help to keep your circulation healthy and reduce the possibility of heart disease.

Check the small print. If you can't read it, you probably need specs. Regular eye checks are a must, as they can pick up on all sorts of problems, such as diabetes, cataracts, glaucoma or cholesterol build-up.

Don't be blighted by bloating. Chew your food thoroughly – a minimum of 20 times, say the experts. The more you chew, the better your body is able to absorb nutrients.

Here's a clever way to lose some pounds – change the cooking method, not the food. Grill rather than fry, steam rather than bake, use lemon juice rather than sauce or dressing.

Look after your back by rearranging cupboards so you aren't always looking for things at floor level in dark corners.

You can't always stop aches and pains, but wearing a copper bracelet may help ease them.

Keep an eye on calcium levels. You need it now more than ever for healthy bones and teeth. Good sources are milk, cheese, curly kale and sesame seeds.

Splash cold water over your eyes every morning to keep them blinking well.

Don't put up with creaky knees. Make sure you eat at least one portion of oily fish a week, such as salmon, sardines and mackerel. They are all rich in omega-3 fatty acids, which are thought to protect against the inflammation that can cause stiff, painful joints.

Start the day well with breakfast. Choose foods that will give you the energy to take you through to lunchtime. Try porridge, homemade muesli, wholemeal toast, eggs, or yogurt with fruit, nuts and seeds.

Cook up a curry full of anti-ageing ingredients including ginger, garlic, chilies, fenugreek seeds, tomatoes, onions and turmeric.

Pack a punch with a pomegranate. The sweet-tasting juice and seeds are full of antioxidant polyphenols, which promote a healthy heart. They may also help protect against prostate and breast cancer.

In traditional Chinese medicine, walnuts are the fruits of longevity. Add walnuts to your snack list or try the oil splashed on salads and in cooking.

Eat more tomatoes to help protect against prostate cancer. Cooked tomatoes and tomato ketchup are rich in a substance called lycopene, which has been shown to offer some protection. Anyone for pizza?

If you can't get to sleep, try a lettuce sandwich. Lettuce contains chemicals with mild sedative powers while the starch in the bread can promote the release of a calming substance in the brain known as serotonin.

Pull up your compression socks up before boarding a plane. It could stop you developing a potentially dangerous blood clot in a vein known as a DVT.

Ditch the Danish, ban the bagel and snack on flax, sesame and sunflower seeds. They're packed full of omega-3 oils, which can help keep joints supple.

Eat early in the evening to allow your stomach plenty of time to digest your meal before you go to bed.

An apple a day can keep the doctor away. It's true. Studies show that apples may help reduce your risk of lung cancer and stroke.

Eat little and often. It helps keep blood levels steady and you'll be less inclined to snack on unhealthy sugary foods.

Pile your plate high with vegetables, fruit, cereals, fish and olive oil as they do in Mediterranean countries. It could reduce your risk of Alzheimer's disease by as much as 40 per cent.

Copy the Chinese and take ginseng. They have used this famous root as a rejuvenating cure-all for more than 5,000 years. It's said to improve memory and mental clarity, especially as we age.

Make red wine your tipple of choice. It contains antioxidants, which have been shown to reduce levels of 'bad' LDL cholesterol and could therefore lessen your risk of heart disease. Up to two glasses a day gives maximum benefit, but watch it – an average glass of wine packs around 95 calories.

Try to graze, not gorge – eat three light meals and several snacks rather than two huge meals. It's kinder on the digestive system as well as helping to keep energy levels on an even keel.

Give your immune system a boost with herbs such as echinacea or astralagus. Ask a naturopath to make you up a dose or buy some at your local health store and follow the instructions on the pack.

Use brown sugar or honey to sweeten hot drinks. White sugar may be more appealing, but it's just empty calories.

Drink at least 8fl oz (250ml) of soya milk, or eat a portion of tofu or soya beans every day. These contain plant hormones known as phytoestrogens, which can help stop bones going brittle.

Get your cholesterol checked at least twice a year, especially if you have a family history of high cholesterol or heart disease.

Broaden your food horizons. If you see something exotic in the supermarket, find out what it is and how to cook it, then give it a go.

Try taking ginkgo. This supplement enhances circulation to the brain, improving cognitive ability, memory and concentration.

If you find you always end up cooking the same meals on the same day each week, it's time to ring the changes. Buy a cookery book, or cut out recipes from magazines and try new dishes to discover new tastes and stimulate your appetite.

Have your health checked regularly. Go for that mammogram, get your prostate checked and keep an eye on cholesterol, blood pressure and blood sugar levels.

Make portion control your mantra. Your metabolism (the rate at which your body burns calories) gradually slows down as you age, so you may find you can't have second helpings without piling on the pounds.

You cannot run away from weakness; you must some time fight it out or perish; and if that be so why not now and where you stand?
ROBERT LOUIS STEVENSON

Go bananas. Full of potassium and natural sugars, they are just the thing for boosting energy levels from dawn to dusk.

Be alternative and embrace preventive medicine. Saw palmetto can help with prostate problems, co-enzyme Q10 may help boost energy levels, and a cup of valerian tea can help with insomnia.

Show your breasts some TLC. TOUCH your breasts. LOOK for changes. Be aware of their shape and texture. CHECK anything unusual with your doctor.

Avoid noisy atmospheres.
Protecting your ears could mean
the difference between having to
wear a hearing aid or not.

*If you can't read the small
print but hate wearing glasses,
ask your optician if you can
try bi-focal contact lenses.*

*Floss your teeth morning and night. It's now
thought that gum disease, if left untreated, can
lead to inflammation of the arteries, and that
could mean heart disease.*

Make one small change at a time. It takes at least three weeks for a new action to become a habit.

Make your cuppa green. Green tea contains higher levels of anti-ageing substances than good old builder's tea.

Think about going veggie. It seems that vegetarians live longer and have a lower risk of heart disease and cancer than their carnivorous peers.

Stop adding salt to your food before tasting it. Too much salt increases blood pressure and is bad for your heart. Check the salt content of packaged food at the supermarket, you'll be surprised how much it contains.

Don't go pop! Too many fizzy drinks can cause calcium to leach from bones, raise blood sugar levels and turn you into a jumpy, irritable fatty.

Pulses have many pluses. They're one of the best sources of roughage, without which your digestion can get sluggish.

Sea vegetables (kelp, wakami, nori and dulse) are the richest source of the minerals you need to keep you fighting fit as you age. These include iodine for a healthy thyroid, chlorine and manganese, which are good for the pituitary gland, and zinc, which can boost the immune system and male fertility.

Start every day with a glass of warm water and lemon juice to help kick-start your liver into action.

Goji berries deserve their accolade of 'happy'. A handful at breakfast is said to keep you smiling for the rest of the day.

Eat your greens, especially spinach and kale. Both are full of eye-friendly chemicals, which will ward off age-related macular degeneration.

Go electric. Using a sonic toothbrush removes up to 15 per cent more plaque than an ordinary one. It can also help protect your gums.

Beware the saturated fats found in cheese, pastry and red meats. Those fats are often the villains behind high cholesterol and heart disease.

Go on a regular mole hunt. Get any that change in any which way checked by your doctor.

Here's how to show your kidneys that you care: drink a mug of warm water and honey, or a glass of cranberry juice, or eat half a medium melon.

Eat organic fruit and veg as much as you can. You'll get more taste, more crunch and more goodness.

Go nuts. They are high in nutrients as well as being a good source of essential unsaturated fatty acids. Just make sure you choose raw unsalted ones for maximum benefit.

Get minted and beat indigestion. A cup of peppermint tea helps digestion and is a good antidote to bloating.

Always meant to give food combining a go? Well, here are the rules. Don't have protein (meat, dairy products, nuts) and starches (potatoes, beans, grains) at the same meal, and always eat fruit by itself.

Soothe travel sickness with ginger. Take one or two capsules of ginger every couple of hours or sip ginger tea.

Taken a tumble? Lessen the trauma and speed up the healing process with arnica cream. But don't use it on broken skin.

> *Health is the second blessing that we mortals are capable of; a blessing that money cannot buy.*
> IZAAK WALTON

Too much caffeine can cause trembling, sweating and headaches, so try fruit and herbal teas instead – there are delicious varieties to choose from now.

If you have had one too many (and who doesn't?), a dose of the herbal remedy milk thistle should soon put you right. It helps to regenerate liver cells and reduce those 'morning after' symptoms.

Take regular screen breaks from computer work for the sake of your eyes. Let your eyes rest on a relaxing sight such as a lush plant or fish in a tank.

Titillate your senses ... all five of them.

• Stimulate your nose with a series of different scents for a few minutes each day to help create new scent receptors.

• If your sense of taste starts to dull, try adding stronger herbs and spices to your cooking.

• Get up early and listen to the dawn chorus.

• Indulge in skin-to-skin contact at least once a day. Hold your partner's or grandchildren's hands at every opportunity, or give your partner a massage.

• Breakfast on bilberries – they're full of antioxidants called anthocyanins that are good for your eyes.

Whittle your waist. Being 'apple' shaped elevates your risk of diabetes and high blood pressure, and raises the level of cholesterol and triglycerides, which in turn increases your risk of heart disease.

Get down to the toyshop and buy a skipping rope. Skipping is good for the bones – any exercise that slightly jars them, helps to build them up and prevent loss of bone density.

Keep your pelvic floor muscles firm. You need strong ones for everything from a happy sex life to avoiding those embarrassing leaks when you run for the bus. Contract them for a count of 10 several times a day.

Did you know that water acts like a giant cushion during exercise? If your creaky knees can't take high-impact exercise, go swimming. Swimming using the crawl action is better than breaststroke, which can actually put strain on the knees.

Tune in to your body as much as you can. If your head hurts or you feel anxious, spend some time discovering why, then deal with the cause.

friends and family

There is no hope of joy except in human relations.
ANTOINE DE SAINT-EXUPÉRY

Those who love deeply never grow old; they may die of old age, but they die young.
DOROTHY CANFIELD FISHER

Recycle to help save the planet for your grandchildren.

Stock up on postcards and stay in touch that way. It makes a change from e-mails and is much more personal.

Plan weekends well ahead. Make a list of people to see, places to go to and things to do. You'll never be at a loose end come Friday night.

Keep as close as you can to friends and family. There's a wealth of evidence that a strong family network boosts immunity, helps protect against illness and may even help you recover faster after an operation.

Speak out about your hopes and expectations for the next few years. Tell your partner and family what you would like to happen during this next phase of your life.

Give your partner space. Even the closest couples need time to themselves, so have some activities you do on your own.

Four hands are better than two. Try to do chores together – they'll be less boring and you should get through them quicker!

Pay a visit to your parents' graves and sit for a while reflecting on happy times you spent together.

Retrace your family history and visit as many significant spots as you can.

Go back to your childhood home:
it will trigger happy memories.

*Spend a day sorting out your
wardrobe with your grandchildren.
They will pounce on things you wore
years ago with cries of 'Vintage!'*

Be a social butterfly. Spending time with
friends and family encourages the release
of immune-boosting feel-good hormones.

> " Friendship is the source of the greatest
> pleasure, and without friends even the most
> agreeable pursuits become tedious. "
>
> ST THOMAS AQUINAS

Invest in a digital camera if you don't already have one. Learn how to upload photos on to your computer and send them to friends and family.

Create an on-line photo album. It's fun to do and your photos will always be at your fingertips.

Is it time to reinvent your social life? Get in touch with friends and past colleagues. Perhaps it's your birthday, Thanksgiving, or midsummer? Use it as an excuse to throw a party.

On the lookout for new friends? Throw yourself into an activity in which people talk to each other, such as acting or cooking. Not all activities, especially classes, are sociable.

Don't say no to invitations. Some people don't ask twice.

Stay away from negative people — they can zap energy and optimism all too fast. Instead, mix with people who inspire you and make you laugh.

Be a good friend – that means listening and not judging.

Treat your friends with respect. Call them if you promised to, and don't take them for granted.

> *Each friend represents a world in us, a world possibly not born until they arrive, and it is only by this meeting that a new world is born.*
> ANAÏS NIN

Be a somebody. Read the newspapers, find out what's going on in the world and have an opinion on current affairs.

Go through old address books and rekindle past friendships. Don't dither – just think how good it would make you feel if someone got in touch with you.

Keep your social circle lively. Join a club or evening class, invite a new friend round for dinner, or go to a different pub.

Try a flower remedy if you find get-togethers tricky:
• Beech if you tend to be critical of others and avoid people because they irritate you.
• Water violet if you find it hard to come out of your shell.

Start a club with other keen swimmers and splash about together once a week.

Don't give up if you want to do something and there isn't a club available locally. Instead, invite friends round and sound them out. There's nothing to stop you starting up your own group.

Forward planning is key. Don't give loneliness a chance to creep in.

Without friends no one would choose to live, though he had all other goods.
ARISTOTLE

If you live on your own or your partner is one of those silent types, get yourself a pet and start talking to it.

Don't cut yourself off from social contact during the day. Walk to the shops. Get to know the postman, newsagent and local traders.

Balance your time between friends, family and yourself. Sometimes being on your own for short periods gives you a better perspective on life.

" *Your best friend is yourself.* "
BOETHIUS

Put photos of friends, family or places you've visited and loved in a spot where you can see them every day.

Learn to delegate – believe it or not, friends and family love to help.

Love something or someone a lot.

Give a present to someone.
Don't wait for birthdays
to make a loved one's day
special. Unexpected gifts
are uplifting for giver and
receiver alike.

Stop being a people-pleaser
and start to please yourself.

Stop being Mum. Remember that however much you love your children, you no longer have to be at their beck and call.

Offer to help with the grandchildren, but be very clear about what you are and are not prepared to do, and when. Don't be coerced into doing more than you can manage.

Grandchildren – you only have them for as long as you want, then you can hand them back!

Take a less active parenting role and a more active grandparenting role.

If you don't see your grandchildren regularly, call, e-mail or text them – they're less likely to be shy when you meet them face to face.

Want to be a hands-on granny? Keep the family home or buy a bigger one and stock up on secondhand cots, high chairs and pushchairs.

Don't want to be a hands-on granny? Sell the family home and buy a one-bed studio as soon as possible.

If you have no children, how about standing in as a parent or grandparent on a voluntary basis? Search on the Internet for organizations looking for surrogate families.

If necessary compromise with friends and family. A little can be better than nothing.

Spend quality time with friends and family. They can help give you that sense of belonging, of being part of something, that you may have taken for granted in the workplace.

Make some new young friends. It will help you keep your finger on the pulse while they will benefit from all your wisdom and experience.

Give friends and family lots of hugs. Touch triggers the release of endorphins, the body's own happy hormones, and makes you and others feel loved.

Build your own website and start a blog to keep friends and family in the picture. Update it daily and upload photos to enhance your story.

Form a book club with local friends.
Take it in turns to choose the title
and become a book critic for a night.

Don't bottle up feelings – this only
aggravates stress. Set up a support
system so there's always someone
there for you to talk to if necessary.

Take your partner on a second honeymoon. Only this time, don't keep the destination a secret.

Revisit places and activities that you and your partner did when you first met. You may not be able to go motor scrambling any more, but you can still go to watch it.

Create a wishing bowl with your partner. Write down sexual and sensual fantasies on slips of paper and pop them in the bowl. Take it in turn to fish out a wish and then act on it.

Couples who keep dating keep mating. Go back to where you first met, return to your old haunts and rekindle memories of the first heady days of your romance.

Be affectionate with your partner. A loving hug, kiss or hand squeeze at the right time can work wonders. An arm around the shoulder or holding hands can mean so much.

Clear the air with a row but never go to bed without making up.

Fire up passion with herbal aphrodisiacs such as muira puama. Derived from the roots and leaves of a Brazilian tree known as potency wood, this is thought to affect the brain chemicals that stimulate nerve endings in the genitals.

Talk to each other and listen to what your partner has to say without butting in. Showing that you care and value what your other half thinks can draw you together and increase desire.

Routine is the enemy of passion. Make it a rule that every time you have sex you do something different, however small.

Make love in the morning or afternoon away, from the bedroom. Who says you have to do it in bed at night?

If sex with your partner has been on the back burner, start slowly so neither of you feels under pressure to perform. Touching, stroking and kissing are good first moves. If you're relaxed and happy with each other, sex will follow naturally.

Setting aside a few minutes each day to focus on each other can help keep you close and clued in to each other's feelings and plans.

Don't always wait for friends to make that call.
Even the closest can drift away if you don't
show you care.

Hold a clothes-swapping
party. It's a great way to
reinvigorate your wardrobe
without spending money.

Contact long-lost cousins. Get them to talk about
your aunts and uncles. You may discover things
about your parents you never knew.

Don't let family feuds fester. Now's the time to sort them out once and for all.

Work out what you are looking for in a friend – if the other person's friendship agenda doesn't match your own, let it go.

Don't get in too deep too quickly – true friendships take time to evolve.

Trace your ancestors and research your family tree on-line with one of the many family tree software packages available.

Get elderly relatives to sit in front of a video or DVD recorder and talk about their past.

Write an account of your life for your children and grandchildren. They can then pass it down the family line.

Single again? Join one of the many online dating agencies to meet potential partners.

Decide exactly what you want from a relationship before you start looking for one, so you can focus on finding that special person who wants similar things.

Keep your family informed if you start to date again. Then they'll be prepared when you decide to introduce them to your new partner.

Use the Internet to widen your circle of friends and support networks at home and abroad.

Join chat rooms and get talking on message boards with like-minded people who share your interests.

Try not to give advice to your children unless you're asked for it. Even then, tread warily. Who likes criticism, especially if it's being dished out by the parents? Like it or not, your children are old enough to run their own lives.

Your life story may seem ordinary to you, but we all have tales to tell. To your family and future descendants, your memories are not only their past but social history.

If you have boxes of old videos, cine films or photos, bring them to life. There are companies on the Internet that will help you restore old photos or transfer them to CD or DVD.

Punctuate your year with weekends away with friends or family. Try to make them at least three days long.

Avoid making a set time each week to visit relatives or children, as they might see a change in routine as a sleight.

Be proactive. This is not the time of life to wait for invitations that may never arrive, so invite yourself.

Even though they're grown up, your children still need to know how much you love and appreciate them. So start telling them now!

" *Love for life creates a loving life.* "
LYNDA FIELD

Reading, studying and sharing your views and opinions with others can help keep your mind stimulated and on a positive track.

Make time for ageing relatives. One day it will be you.

Visit www.friendsreunited.com or Google the names of school friends. It can be fascinating to find out what they look like and are doing now.

"There is no friend
Like a sister
In calm or stormy weather;
To cheer one on the tedious way,
To fetch one if one goes astray,
To lift one if one totters down,
To strengthen whilst one stands."
CHRISTINA ROSSETTI

*put your house
in order*

Tidy up. Whittle down paperwork – label and file. Include bank and building society passbooks, chequebooks, details of investments, and so on.

Loose pieces of paper get lost and forgotten. Buy yourself a folder or organizer and keep them together in one place.

Make a list of paid advisers (including addresses and phone numbers) such as lawyers, accountants, life insurance agents, financial advisers and so on, and file it away.

Throw away any embarrassing bits and bobs that you wouldn't want your loved ones to discover. Yes, that includes the box of letters from your lover of the past 20 years whom your partner doesn't know about.

Adopt a clear-desk policy. Aim to handle each piece of paper just once. This means dealing with bills, forms and so on immediately, then filing them away.

Be e-mail efficient. Check your in-box regularly but answer e-mails only at specific times. Then you can choose which e-mails to prioritize rather than dealing with each one as it arrives.

Junk the junk. You don't have to keep answering the phone to kitchen salespeople – just register online at a telephone preference service. Here, you can join a register to say that you do not wish to receive unsolicited sales and marketing calls.

Register for Internet banking. You can check your balance, transfer money, apply for an overdraft, pay bills and make credit card payments 24 hours a day. Online saving accounts often have high rates for silver savers.

Choose pin numbers that you'll remember easily, such as your cat's birthday, and never disclose them to anyone.

Be a pay pal. Sign up to
www.paypal.com and you can
buy online without having to spend
time searching for your credit card
number and financial information
every time you make a purchase.

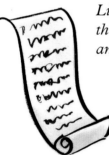

*Live by the list – you won't forget
things and it will help you prioritize
and also keep to your priorities.*

Declutter your life. For each item, ask
yourself, 'Do I really use it? Do I really love
it?' If the answer is no, take it to a charity
shop or recycle it at www.freecycle.com.

Do your sums. Now's the time for some financial planning. Work out what kind of lifestyle you can realistically afford with the funds you have.

Whenever you invest, remember the basics: don't put money into something that's hard to understand, research before buying and go for quality and safety.

Don't be rash with savings. Seek advice before committing yourself to any moneymaking schemes, however tempting. Remember that it's hard to recoup money lost at this stage of life.

Set up a rainy day fund to provide for unexpected bills. The boiler might blow up, your kitchen could be flooded or your car may give up the ghost.

Find out all you can about your pension and annuities, and seek expert advice on maximizing your retirement income.

Guard against identity fraud by taking care when throwing away financial documents such as bank statements and credit card bills. Shred or burn!

If you need additional income, consider a part-time job. Running a business from home or working for a supermarket are possibilities.

Reduce the worry about how those bills are going to be paid. Install Microsoft Money on your computer (if you have one). This way you can set up a personal finance programme that will help you devise a budget and track your expenses.

If you need or want to carry on working, do some networking. Tell everyone you know and meet that you are job hunting. Order some business cards and get out there.

> *If you don't fly first class your children will.*
> LUFTHANSA ADVERTISEMENT

Pay extra for the hotel room overlooking the sea. The chances are you'll remember the wonderful view for far longer than the outrageous bill.

Take a taxi if you feel tired. Look on it as a way of conserving energy rather than an indulgence.

Be generous to family and friends if you can afford it. Think how much more satisfying it is to see the pleasure that presents can bring, rather than imagining how it might be after you're gone.

It may be time to move. Is your house too big? Are there too many stairs for the years ahead? How close is it to family and friends? These are the things you need to start thinking about now.

How about a house swap? Look up professional house-swapping companies on the Internet. Alternatively, could you do a deal with overseas friends? Make sure your home insurance is in order in case of mishaps and maybe ask for a deposit.

Retire abroad. Property is cheaper, it costs less to live and the sun shines! Retirement hotspots include Portugal, Spain and France.

If you decide you want to move overseas, why not rent somewhere first for a few months? That way, you can find out what living there is really like before committing yourself.

THINGS TO DO NOW THAT YOU'RE RETIRED

Your house needs updating but you'd rather not move? Giving it a quick makeover can be really uplifting. Magazines and TV shows are full of ideas. If you can afford it, why not get an interior designer to hold your hand?

If you want to keep your house but can't afford to, look at equity release schemes. These allow you to draw down capital or raise income against your home without having to move. Always seek expert advice from a financial adviser.

Do you have medical insurance and if so does the premium need topping up? Check the small print and make sure you're covered for every eventuality.

If you have dependants, take out life assurance. Even if it's for only a small amount, at least that way they will have enough to tide them over in the short term.

Find out what retirement benefits you and your family are entitled to and make sure you get your due.

The only thing we have to fear is fear itself.
FRANKLIN DELANO ROOSEVELT

Buy some premium bonds. Winnings are tax-free and that surprise cheque in the post can really brighten up the day.

Take a positive attitude to your retirement and you'll increase your chances of enjoying this phase of life when you have more time for yourself.

> Retirement is wonderful. It's doing nothing without worrying about getting caught at it.
> GENE PERRET

Be proud of your achievements and don't dwell on past mistakes that can't be undone. Look to the future with optimism. Enjoy the challenges that every new day brings.

If you're considering a retirement home, think carefully about the type of property you want, the location and whether you're likely to move again. Visit several before making up your mind.

Make a will and leave it somewhere easy to find. If you don't, your belongings won't go where you want them to and it could take an age before they go anywhere at all. Worse still, the state will probably claim the best part of them.

Homemade wills can be open to misinterpretation. Avoid a future family fall-out and use a solicitor.

Make a comprehensive list of what you want to leave and to whom. Include addresses and phone numbers if necessary.

If you have too many things to list independently and decide to leave your belongings in equal shares to your children make sure you stipulate how they're divided up. That way, there is no room for argument. For example, the person who has first choice, or whether lots should be drawn for coveted items.

Make a separate list of the history of your belongings and head it 'Provenance'. Your granddaughter might like to know that the necklace she has inherited once belonged to Great-Aunt Mildred.

Update your will regularly. You need to keep it in sync with rising property prices, the current state of your investments, and so on.

It might be wise to give your family as much of their inheritance as you can during your lifetime to prevent it being snatched by the taxman.

Make provisions for pets. Who do you want to look after your budgie if you're suddenly rushed to hospital?

Think about drawing up a living will in case you become so ill that you can't make decisions about your care. Would you want to be resuscitated, for example?

Fast forward to your funeral. What songs or hymns do you want? And how about readings? If you can bear to think about it, you can make sure your family and friends send you off just the way you want.

You can decide what goes on your headstone: make it as light-hearted or serious as you like. Winston Churchill's read 'I am ready to meet my maker. Whether my maker is ready to meet me is another matter.' Spike Milligan's read 'I told you I was ill.'

Think about organ donation. If you want to give life to others, register your wishes and carry a donor card.

> They say such nice things about people at their funerals that it makes me sad that I'm going to miss mine by just a few days.
>
> GARRISON KEILLOR

Decide if you want to be buried or cremated, or go the green way with a woodland funeral. You can look on the Internet for the many options available.

Make your wishes known to friends and family in case you need future help and support. If you fall ill they may not find it easy to second-guess you.

You can't take it with you, so don't keep too tight a hold on the purse strings. It's OK to spend some of your savings if it will make your life today more comfortable.

" Age is a state of mind, not a number. "
BELINDA SEPER

the inner you

> Your vision will become clear only when you can look into your own heart. Who looks outside dreams; who looks inside awakens.
>
> CARL JUNG

Let go of the sensible grown-up within you and enjoy the freedom that comes from being able to forget about work at last.

What you believe about life, death and spirituality shapes your outlook. There is no right or wrong belief, but if you know what you believe you'll achieve inner peace.

Write your obituary. It need not be as morbid as it sounds. Writing an account of your achievements can be a positive experience. The only thing that will be missing is what you still intend to do.

> *Retirement requires the invention of a new hedonism, not a return to the hedonism of youth.*
> MASON COOLEY

Investigate body therapies that work on releasing old emotions and traumas. Try rolfing, biodynamic massage or radionics.

Don't worry about talking to yourself. See it as a form of self-expression rather than the first sign of madness.

Let go of the past. You can't change it. Now's the time to move into the future, starting today.

Don't fret about giving up work. It's bound to feel strange initially, but you'll soon get used to it and see how much life still holds for you.

Be a human being rather than a human doing. Relax with yoga, meditation or deep-breathing exercises.

Religion can be comforting and a source of strength through difficult periods.

Think about going to a church, temple, mosque or synagogue service. Shared worship provides a community that will nourish your soul and nurture your faith and hope, as well as giving you the opportunity to make new friends.

Whether you are a believer or not, go on a retreat. It will give you some silent moments for peaceful thought.

Worrying will never get you anywhere, so stop now. Write down your worries in order of their importance. Sometimes just seeing them on paper helps you to consider them in a different light.

Make sure you have at least one activity in your life that nourishes your soul. It may be gardening, painting, music or just helping others.

Collect some inspirational sayings and refer to them whenever you feel in need of motivation. Put them on pretty cards on your bathroom mirror, fridge, computer — wherever they will catch your eye.

Other people do not have the power to ruin your day. Only your thoughts have the power to do that.

Start dreaming about your successful retirement, but make sure it's your dream and not someone else's.

Escape the outside world by concentrating on your breathing for a few moments each day. Sit still with your back straight, close your eyes and start to focus on the rise and fall of your breath.

You can't turn the clock back so look ahead and make sure you really do what you want to do now.

If you have a problem, addiction, fear or phobia that you want to be free of, why not tackle it now? Try hypnotherapy or cognitive behavioral therapy (CBT).

How about some soul-searching therapies such as rebirthing or past life therapy? These can be very powerful in a positive way.

> *A man is but the product of his thoughts: what he thinks he becomes.*
> *MAHATMA GANDHI*

Spend a day really listening to everyone you meet, rather than talking and only half-listening to them.

Learn how to meditate and give some time to it every day. It will keep you calm and can help bring spiritual fulfilment.

Nurture inner peace with a session in a flotation tank. If you want stillness and silence, avoid those with piped whale music.

Understand that doing nothing is not a waste of time, but being unhappy about doing nothing is.

Learn to appreciate your life – the downs and the ups. The downs make the ups seem even more wonderful.

Think about the person you would most like to spend time with – and then work towards becoming that person.

If you believe that you can do a thing or if you believe that you cannot, in either case you are right.
HENRY FORD

Trust your intuitive voice. The keys to awareness are within you.

If you had just four weeks to live, what would you say to whom? Say it now. Live as if there is no tomorrow because there may not be one.

If you were brought up as a practising believer, why not try returning to your faith? You may find in it things you couldn't find when you were young.

Who is always there in the good times and the bad? You. When in doubt about anything, look inside yourself. You have all the answers.

Direct your energy and attention inwards. Listen to yourself and work out how you really feel (not what you would like to feel or think you should feel). Try to quieten your mind and listen to your inner self.

Think about what is really important to you, then spend some time every day doing things that help reinforce your own personal values.

Try to make peace with yourself and others. Let go of any long-held grudges and resentments about both people and life in general.

Are there things that are coming between you and your dreams? Now is the time to remove them if you are ever going to fulfil your potential.

If you are worried about the future and what it may hold, voice your fears with a close friend. Often, talking about concerns helps to dispel them.

Explore new spiritual avenues and philosophies of life. There may be some life-changing things in them for you.

Keep a dream diary and see if you can identify any recurring patterns. Think about them and what they could mean. Perhaps they are trying to tell you something.

 If my mind can conceive it, and my heart can believe it, I know I can achieve it.
REVEREND JESSE JACKSON

Belief is the most powerful magic of all.
LYNDA FIELD

You may not be responsible for all the things that have gone wrong in your life, but you are responsible for doing something about them.

Now is the time to recognize once and for all that you can only change yourself, not others. Accept what you can't change and you will feel much happier.

Bitterness is toxic. Don't let it poison you.

*Don't ever give up –
keep striving towards
your goals. It isn't over
until the final whistle.*

" *A dream is a wish your heart makes.* "
WALT DISNEY

Don't worry about tomorrow. Learn to be content and happy with the here and now.

Take a mental mini-break. Close your eyes, think of a beautiful scene and fill it with as much detail as you can. Focus on these thoughts for 10 to 15 minutes, then slowly let the image go.

Discover what you really want by looking at the lives of those who seem happy and fulfilled.

Make sure there's plenty of passion in your life. You need it to fire up your soul and keep your mind alive and alert.

> *If you can laugh every day especially at yourself, you've found the best joke in the world.*
> LORETTA LAROCHE

Say what you mean and mean what you say. It allows you to be true to your inner self and makes life a whole lot easier — both for yourself and the people around you.

There's only so much luggage you can take on a plane – and the same can be applied to life. Get rid of any baggage that's weighing you down. You'll look better, feel lighter and have more room in the suitcase for new things.

If you find yourself dwelling on what you haven't achieved, stop it now. Instead, concentrate on all the good things in your life and learn to be grateful.

If you want to find a deeper meaning to life, there's no point looking around you. The only place you will find it is deep inside yourself.

Remember that everything you have gone through has brought you to where you are now. Make sure that what you do and think in retirement leads you to where you want to be.

"You're always alone, but you're only lonely if you don't like the person you're alone with. Try to love yourself a little more each day – loving starts with the self."

DR WAYNE W. DYER

Take some risks. You may fail from time to time, but you will go on learning from the experience.

Don't get upset if you have a memory hiccup. Relax and you may be surprised – you will eventually remember what you had forgotten.

" Just slow down and enjoy it all. "
DR WAYNE W. DYER

An Hachette Company
First Published in Great Britain in 2005 by Spruce,
a division of Octopus Publishing Company Ltd
Endeavour House, 189 Shaftesbury Avenue, London, WC2H 8JY
www.octopusbooks.co.uk
www.octopusbooksusa.com

Distributed in the U.S. and Canada for Octopus Books USA
c/- Hachette Book Group USA
237 Park Avenue
New York, NY 10017

ISBN: 978-1-84601-243-3

10 9 8 7

Printed and bound in China.